KU-067-852

THE NATIONAL TRUST

# Investigating FOOD in HISTORY

## By Lisa Chaney
### Illustrated by Virginia Westmacott

## Contents

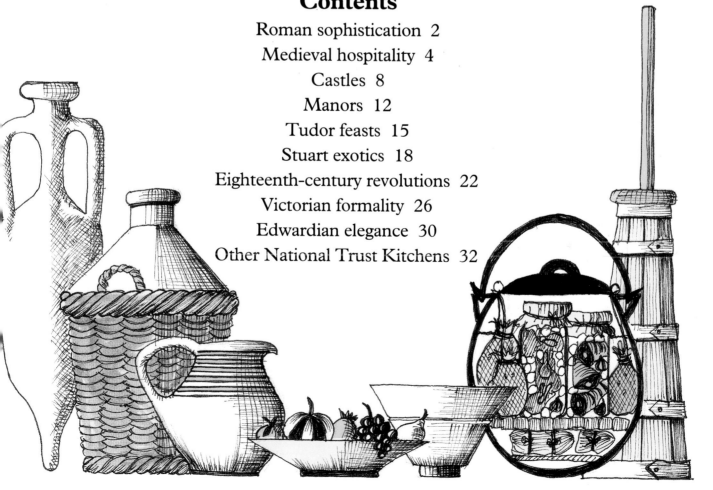

# Roman sophistication

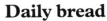

By 43 AD Britain was part of the Roman Empire. The food enjoyed by the Romans was more sophisticated and varied than that of the early Britons, who ate coarse bread, drank dark ale and occasionally indulged in cannibalism.

In southern Britain particularly, large farmhouses were built for the wealthy Romans who came to rule. **Chedworth Villa** in Gloucestershire, built in about 120 AD, was one of these large farming complexes.

## Grow your own

The family in this villa would have lived in great comfort and eaten well. In carefully laid out kitchen gardens, fruit, vegetables and herbs not previously seen in Britain were grown by slave gardeners: mulberries, apples, pears and cherries (wild ones grew here already); onions, leeks, carrots, cucumbers, asparagus, turnips and radishes, and a variety of salad crops; dill, borage, fennel, garlic, mint, parsley, sage, marjoram and thyme.

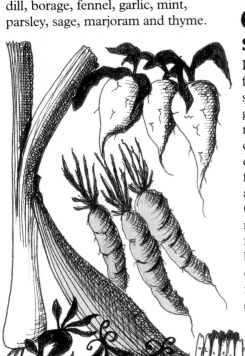

## Spices and oils

In such a wealthy household, recipes for both meat and sweet dishes used spices like cinnamon, nutmeg and ginger. Olive oil from the European mainland was used in sauces, dressings and for frying. Imported dried fruits such as raisins, dates and figs were enjoyed both in meat dishes and as desserts by the family at Chedworth. The household slaves meanwhile existed on much simpler foods. Porridges of cereal and coarse bread formed the major part of their diet, enlivened with only a little meat.

## Daily bread

Roman farming methods were more advanced than those of the Britons they had conquered. Wheat, barley and rye were grown for bread. The remains of ovens constructed of rubble and tiles in the shape of low beehives can still clearly be seen at Chedworth. A coarse, dark bran and wheat loaf (**autopyron**) was made for the slaves and dogs, whilst barley bread was given as punishment rations to soldiers. **Athletae** was bread mixed with soft curd cheese and **artophites** was a light bread made from the finest wheat flour.

## A Roman recipe: Isicium

This Roman version of an omelette made with sheep's brains was a common dish for lunch.

Soak brains in cold water and leave for 7 – 10 minutes.
Blend pepper, lovage and origan in liquamen (see page 3).
Mix up the brains, spices and liquamen with eggs and beat until smooth. Cook in a very low fire, until completely set.
Turn out onto a chopping board and cut into one inch squares.

## Larger than life

A great variety of meat and fish would have been eaten at Chedworth. Rabbits, mice and even snails were fattened up first. Guinea fowl, peacocks and pheasants were introduced into Britain. Sheep, goats and cattle were popular both as meat and as a source of milk, which was then usually made into cheese. Pork was a favourite with soldiers and lard formed part of their daily rations. Deer, wild boar and bear were hunted and small wild birds were caught in nets.

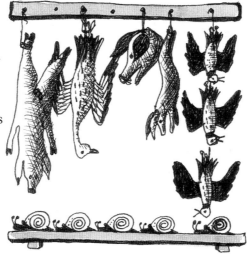

## Utensils

Food in the villa kitchens was prepared by slaves using utensils made from wood, bone, iron, or bronze. Much of the cooking was done over a raised brick hearth containing a charcoal fire. Pots and pans stood over this on tripods or gridirons.

## Liquid substances

Two substances of great importance in the Chedworth kitchens were wine and **liquamen (garum)**. Liquamen was made from fish, the insides of larger fish and a lot of salt, either left to ferment in the sun or boiled up together and then strained. The resulting sticky substance was something like anchovy essence, or very strong Worcester sauce, and was used in everything from meat stews to sweet puddings! Wine was imported in bulk in wooden barrels or clay storage jars **(amphorae)**. Some grapes were grown in Britain; most were made into verjuice, the sharp, slightly fermented juice of sour grapes that was used in cookery rather like vinegar would be today.

## And so to eat...

The dining-room **(triclinium),** where the family took their meals, would have contained three low couches arranged in a U-shape around the table. To eat they reclined on their left side and stretched for food and drink with their right hand. Forks were unknown and knives and spoons rarely used, so most Romans ate with their fingers. They did use finger bowls and sometimes white napkins were spread protectively over the edge of the couch. The three meals of the day were breakfast **(ientaculum)** of bread and fruit; lunch **(prandium)** of cold meat, egg or fish with vegetables and bread; and dinner, the main meal of the day **(cena)**, consisting of three courses.

**3**

# Medieval hospitality

By 407 AD the last of the Roman soldiers had left Britain, returning to Rome to try to defend it against invaders. Gradually the towns and forts they had built were destroyed and overrun by Angles, Saxons, Jutes, and in the north, Picts and Scots. Roman ways were forgotten and for hundreds of years most people went back to living and eating as they had before the Romans came.

When in 1066 the Normans conquered England, the new king, William I, set up a system of estates. Each estate was an almost self-sufficient unit with peasants or villeins working the land for their lord.

## Monasteries

Though they were fierce warriors, the Normans were devout Christians and founded many new monasteries. **Fountains Abbey** in Yorkshire was one of these, founded by the Cistercian Order in 1135.

The Cistercian monks lived by strict rules, promising to lead a simple and disciplined life. Seven church services a day were interspersed with work, reading and meals. In summer there were two meals a day: dinner at 11am and supper at 6.45pm. In winter there was only one meal, dinner, served at 1.45pm. The Abbot could allow extra meals when it was very cold.

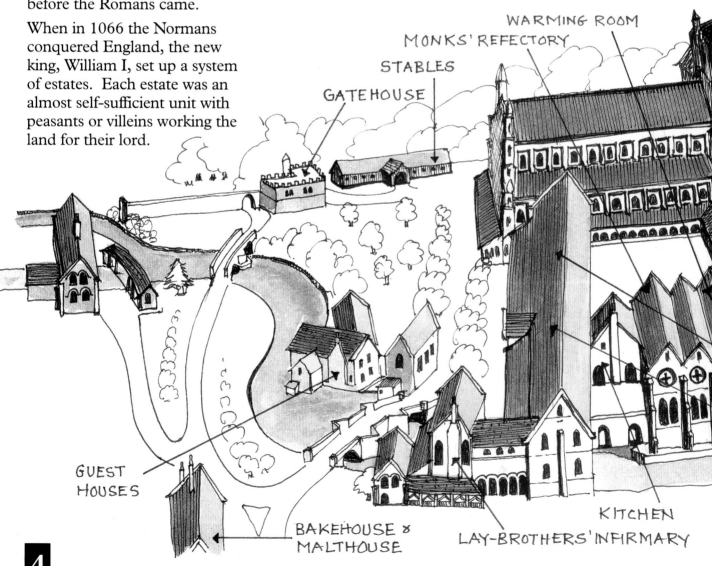

WARMING ROOM

MONKS' REFECTORY

STABLES

GATEHOUSE

GUEST HOUSES

BAKEHOUSE & MALTHOUSE

LAY-BROTHERS' INFIRMARY

KITCHEN

## Bread and water

Large walled vegetable gardens, orchards and many acres of surrounding fields provided the monks with their food. Corn and other cereals used for bread were stored in enormous barns like the one at **Buckland Abbey** in Devon.

Fountains Abbey is situated by a river, as were most monasteries, in order to run the mill to grind the corn for bread, and as a source of fresh fish.

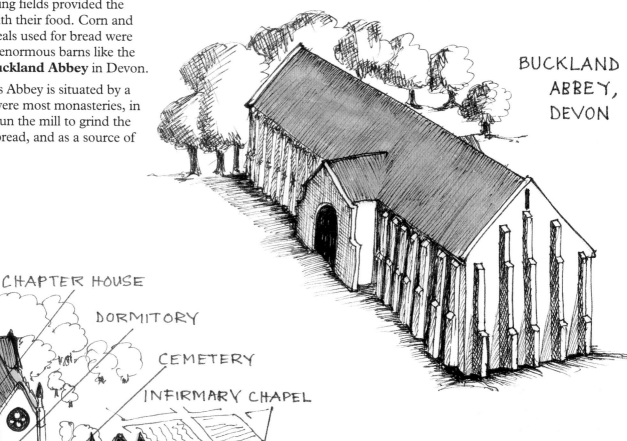

BUCKLAND ABBEY, DEVON

CHAPTER HOUSE

DORMITORY

CEMETERY

INFIRMARY CHAPEL

INFIRMARY

ABBOT'S HOUSE

REREDORTER

LAY-BROTHERS' DORMITORY

LAY BROTHERS' REFECTORY

## Rules and regulations

Originally the monks were forbidden to eat the meat of four-footed creatures, though fish and occasionally pigeons were eaten in small quantities. The main diet was simply of beans, root vegetables, bread and occasionally cheese. Animal meat was given only to the sick or elderly, eaten in a special room called the **misericord** (room of mercy), set near the **infirmary** (sick-room) and away from the **refectory** (dining room). Gradually these rules became less strict.

## A medieval recipe:
### Vegetable and herb salad

Medieval monks would have eaten a lot of fresh vegetables and herbs, grown in the monastery gardens. This salad comes from an old medieval recipe book, written in the late fourteenth century, called the *The Boke of Nuture* – how many of the herbs and vegetables can you recognise?

'Take parsal, sawge, garlec, chibollas, oynons, leek, borage, myntes, porrectes, fenel, and ton tressis, rew, rosemarye, purslayne, lave and waisshe hem clene. Pike hem, pluk hem small with thyn hond and myng hem wel with rawe oile. Lay on vynegar and salt and serve it forth.'

Here are some ingredients you could use to make a medieval-style salad:

| | |
|---|---|
| spring onions | parsley |
| leeks | sage |
| baby onions | borage |
| large onions | mint |
| fennel | watercress |
| garlic | rosemary |

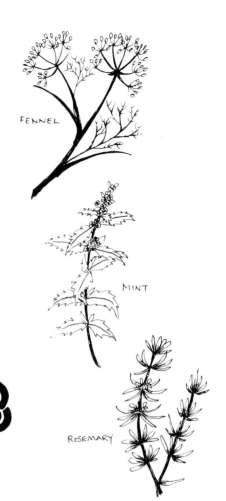

FENNEL

MINT

ROSEMARY

## Blood suckers

Doctors at this time thought that it was good for your health to 'let blood' regularly, taken from the patient usually by applying blood-sucking leeches. After the letting, the monk would be given a restorative dish of parsley, sage and soft eggs.

## Drink

Water was seldom drunk as it was often unclean. Instead, ale was made in the large brewhouse from barley with freshly drawn well water. As much as fifty barrels every ten days, each barrel containing thirty-six gallons of ale, could be produced at Fountains Abbey. Later, cider was made from apples too.

# Who's who

The Cellarer, who supervised all storage and production of food and drink, had many monks and lay brothers working under him. The Kitchener took charge of cooking fuel and staffing the kitchen, supervised the growing of apples for cider-making, and the beehives for honey. As sugar had to be imported from North Africa it was scarce and costly, so honey would be used as the principal sweetener in cooking. Beeswax for candles also came from the hives.

The Refectorer was in charge of serving and clearing away meals and providing washing facilities beforehand.

Speaking was forbidden in the refectory (in fact the monks spent most of their time in silence). While they ate, they listened to religious readings from the pulpit, the base of which can still be seen on the wall at Fountains Abbey.

The Almoner looked after the poor of the neighbourhood. Every day they came to the monastery, were given black rye bread, ale and leftovers from the monastery tables. Visiting dignitaries, merchants and ordinary travellers, who were permitted to stay in the guesthouse, were usually entertained at the Abbot's table where wine and meat would be served.

**Other National Trust monasteries:**

Lacock Abbey, Wiltshire

Hailes Abbey, Gloucestershire

Anglesey Abbey, Cambridgeshire

Buckland Abbey, Devon

# Castles

In the castles and manor houses scattered around England in the Middle Ages, there was great specialisation of domestic tasks, just as in the monasteries.

In 1388 at **Bodiam** in Sussex, Sir Edward Dalyngrigge built one of the last medieval castles in England to protect the area from French invasions and to demonstrate his wealth and power. This castle formed the headquarters of his great household, with up to one hundred people to feed. The household would be almost entirely male, with the exception of Sir Edward's wife and daughters and their personal servants.

## Eating on a grand scale

The largest and most important room of the castle was the Great Hall. There are, in fact, two halls at Bodiam: one for the higher ranking members of the household who lived in the castle; the other for the labourers working on the estate. When in residence, Sir Edward dined every day in the former with his family and household; when he wished to entertain distinguished guests more privately he would use the Great Chamber on an upper floor of the castle.

At the east end of the Great Hall, on a slightly raised platform (**dais**), was the high table for the family and

their chief guests. Running down either side of the Hall were set tables for the household and less important guests, in descending order of rank. Under the customary 'Laws of Hospitality' the host, be he Lord or Abbot, was expected to provide food and shelter for passing travellers.

Across the other end of the room stood a screen with a gallery above, where music could be performed. At feasts the musicians sounded a fanfare to announce the arrival of each new course.

Behind the screen was a passage with doors leading to the buttery, pantry, kitchen and cellars.

## Domestic duties

In the buttery (French for bottling place is **bouttelerie**) wine and ale was dispensed by the butler. The pantry (French for bread store is **painetterie**) was run by the pantler. The kitchen was supervised by the chief cook, with help from assistants and scullions. Scullions were young boys who did all the most basic jobs, including washing-up using sand and slightly soapy herbs like soapwort, and turning the spits across the fires to roast the meat.

At Bodiam, behind the kitchen, stairs led down to the huge well, eight feet in diameter and ten feet deep, which supplied water for the castle. More stairs led up to a pigeon or dove loft which contained about 300 nesting boxes. These birds provided an important part of the castle's year-round meat supply. The larder and cellar stored all other foods and, as in the monastery, were run by the cellarer. He had to store enough food to withstand a potential siege. At Bodiam he was also responsible for hiring servants and overall management of the home farm, beyond the moat. Here animals were reared to produce meat and dairy produce for the castle table. Grain for bread was grown on the surrounding estate fields by Sir Edward's labourers, while vegetables, herbs and fruit were grown in gardens within the castle walls. Like the medieval monastery, the castle was an almost self-sufficient community.

## Meal times

Three meals were eaten each day: breakfast of bread and ale at daybreak; dinner between 11 and 12am; and supper at 5pm.

## Place settings

Before dinner, the pantler would lay the high table with linen cloths and set the great silver-gilt covered bowl for salt (called the cellar, because it stored the salt) in front of Sir Edward's place. The pantler would also lay warm bread rolls in an elaborately folded white napkin (shoes, water lilies and fleurs-de-lis were favourite shapes), a knife and a spoon (forks were still unknown at this time). Trenchers were made by cutting large brown bread loaves a few days old into thick slices to be used as plates. At the high table several of these would be used for each meal, whilst those lower in rank might have only one or two. The pantler would then set the other tables with trenchers and plain salt cellars.

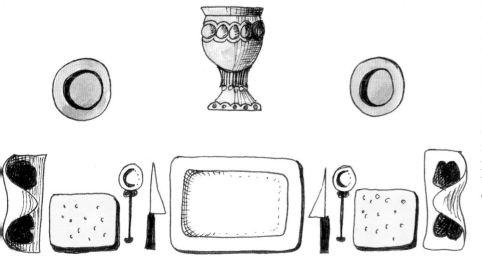

## A medieval recipe to make:

### Honey toasts with pine nuts

This sweet dish would only have been eaten by the rich as honey and pine nuts were expensive. It was first invented for the Coronation Feast of Henry IV in 1399.

225g (8oz) stiff honey

A pinch of ground ginger

A pinch of back pepper

4 large square slices of white bread (no crusts) about 1cm thick

15g (½ oz) pine nut kernels

Put honey, spices and pepper in a small saucepan over a very low heat. Melt the honey and simmer for not more than 2 minutes. Do not let the honey boil or darken, or it will start turning to toffee. Let it cool slightly. Meanwhile, toast the bread lightly on both sides. Cut each slice into 4 small squares. Place on a heated serving plate and pour the syrupy honey over them. Then stick pine kernels in each piece and eat while hot.

## Senior servants

The head of the Hall servants was the Steward, who took charge of the castle when Sir Edward was away. The chief official at dinner was the Marshal and under him were many other servants. One of the most important of these was the Carver, who skillfully carved the many varieties of meat, from swan and peacock to beef and porpoise, in front of the assembled company. Each animal, bird or fish was carved in a particular way, each with its own verb: 'slat a pike; spoil a hen; disfigure a peacock; border a pastry'.

## Sotelte

A piece of highly-coloured sugar paste sculpture, perhaps depicting Diana, the Roman goddess of hunting, having shot her arrow at a stag, surrounded by her pack of hunting dogs. One of the ladies present might be asked to pull the arrow from the stag's belly and blood (actually wine) would come pouring out, to the delight of all present.

## Dining in the Great Hall

Dinner was divided into two courses, with dessert afterwards for those on the high table on special occasions. Each course consisted of several different types of dish served up at the same time – meats, vegetables and sweet things all put on together. Highly coloured foods were popular, using substances such as saffron, saunders (powdered sandalwood), spinach and parsley juice.

Those at the high table were served first with the choicest pieces. Dip-in sauces in 'saucers' were put on the table, while pages stood by with basins of water and towels for regular washing of hands. Those at the lower tables were handed the platters and served themselves.

Only the lord of the manor was served individually. Other people ate in pairs if only one side of the table was occupied, or in fours if there were people sitting on both sides. Food was divided into portions or 'messes' beforehand and two or four people then ate from a platter together, transferring a portion onto their own trenchers using a knife, spoon or most often their fingers. At the end of each course the trenchers were collected up and sometimes given to the poor. Towards the end of the fifteenth century bread trenchers began to be replaced by wooden boards with a special little hole in which to place salt. At the end of the meal, **hippocras** (sweetened, spiced wine) and **wafers** (thin discs of delicately flavoured biscuit) were often served to the high table.

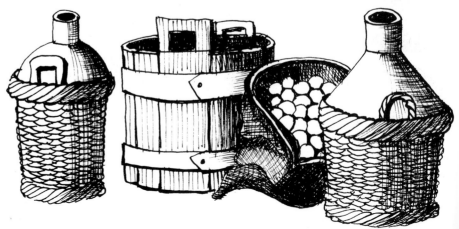

## Mind your manners

This shared way of eating called for everyone to be as clean and considerate as possible. Instructions on table manners were written down for young people in etiquette books. They were told 'not to put chewed bones back on the shared plate, but to throw them on the floor for the dogs; not to prowl around your head looking for lice, nor to pick your nose or blow it on the tablecloth. You are not to use your mouth to squirt or belch or hiccough. Do not slurp your soup and do not pat the dog. But above all, you must always beware of your hinder parts from guns blasting [farting].'

## Cookery books

The oldest usable cookery book, **The Forme of Cury**, was written by the chief cooks to Richard II, in the 1390s, at about the same time that Bodiam was being built. Manuscripts like this would only have been used in wealthy households. Few people could read or write, so most recipes were passed on by word of mouth.

### Other National Trust castles:

Dunster Castle, Somerset

Compton Castle, Devon

Tattershall Castle, Lincolnshire

Corfe Castle, Dorset

Croft Castle, Hereford and Worcester

Chirk Castle, Clwyd

# Manors

Just as monasteries and castles in the Middle Ages were large communities with many mouths to feed, so, on a slightly smaller scale, were manor houses which usually had a large estate to cater for almost all domestic needs. A good example of this type of house is **Cotehele** in Cornwall, built by the Edgcumbe family in the fifteenth and sixteenth centuries.

Walled gardens around the house would have sections for vegetables, herbs and fruit. Poultry and rabbits were usually kept within the walls too.

## Dairy produce

On the estate's home farm the dairy produced a variety of cheese: hard cheese (made from skimmed milk); soft cheese (cream cheese made from whole milk and matured for only a short time); and green cheese (a fresh curd cheese drained on beds of straw or nettles). If herbs were added, then the cheese would be called 'spermyse'.

Junket was a special form of green cheese made from cream curdled with rennet (the digestive juice in the stomach of young animals such as calves, kids and lambs). The name junket comes from the Old French for little rush baskets, **jonquettes**, in which the cheese was drained in France. Sugar, rosewater and spices were added to make the junket into a delicious, rich dish to be eaten at the end of the meal. Custards were also popular, made of combinations of eggs, cream, milk, sugar, cloves, ginger, nutmeg, rosewater and decorated with dates or currants. Dairy products were called 'white meats'.

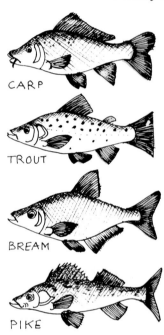

CARP

TROUT

BREAM

PIKE

## Fish days

On Wednesdays, Fridays and Saturdays plus special religious days the Church forbad everyone to eat meat. These were called 'fish days' as opposed to meat days or 'flesh days'. Unless fresh fish was available, this meant eating salted and pickled herring, or stockfish – dried cod from Norway which was so hard it had to be beaten with a stick before it was cooked.

At Cotehele, Sir Richard Edgcumbe held the fishing rights to the river, so the only way the villagers could have the fish was by poaching. A 'kiddle', a large fish trap set across the river, was strictly illegal, and anyone caught using one was severely punished.

## Stew pond

A pond, called a stew, would be dug and stocked with carp and pike. At **Cotehele** the nearby River Tamar also provided a plentiful supply of fish such as trout, grayling, tench and bream.

## Implements

People would bring their own knife and spoon (together called a **nef**) to the table. These were carried in a sheath hanging on their belt. Ladies had embroidered sheaths, often given to them as wedding presents. Forks were used only for serving. Toothpicks for the wealthy were made of precious metals and were often carried stuck in their hats.

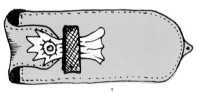

MAN'S NEF

LADY'S NEF

## Winter food

Through the winter, as the farm animals' fodder ran out, they were gradually slaughtered, leaving only the most healthy for breeding the following spring. Some joints were eaten straightaway, others were smoked by hanging them from the meat rack above the fire in the kitchen, or salted by being stored away in great barrels between layers of salt. In order to eat this salt meat, it had to be soaked in water, with straw or oatmeal added to remove the salt taste.

The dovecote at Cotehele housed great numbers of doves and pigeons, a very useful extra supply of winter meat. Inside the dovecote is a 'potence', a revolving ladder for easier access to the higher pigeon holes.

The favoured way to cook meat was roasting on a spit over the fire. A huge drip pan was placed underneath to catch the fat for basting. Everything from little birds to whole lambs, sides of beef, deer or a wild boar, could be cooked in this way. Roasted joints were carved from the spit, brought straight to the table, and handed round from the point of the knife.

## Hunting

Beef and mutton from the home farm were regularly eaten, but a wide variety of game animals and birds were hunted for the table too. Like river fish, game animals at Cotehele were the property of Sir Richard and poaching could be punishable by death.

## Fires for cooking

Until the mid-fourteenth century almost all fires, whether for heating a room or for cooking, were in the middle of the room, with a hole in the roof to allow the smoke to escape. In the late fourteenth century better-off households began to move their fireplaces to a side wall with a chimney above. A cauldron could then be hung over the fire on a pot hanger fixed in the chimney. When sea coal began to replace wood in the sixteenth century, wrought-iron fire baskets on legs were put in fireplaces to provide the greater updraught needed by coal.

## Beans

The basis of the everyday diet was starchy food such as bread and beans. Beans formed the basis of the many different recipes for pottage, a kind of porridge eaten by everyone, rich or poor, and to which a variety of herbs, spices, vegetables and meat (if you were lucky) were added. From this we get the sayings 'I don't give a bean' and 'I haven't got a bean.'

For richer people the bread was of better quality. From the thirteenth century the name 'manchet' was applied to white bread of the finest quality eaten by the gentry. The word is thought to have come from the French **manger**. It was made from wheat flour sifted or bolted two or three times through fine cloths. These breads were actually wholemeal with the coarse bran removed, and they were not white but yellow. Poorer people ate brown bread, often with the addition of rye, barley, or even peas or beans when times were bad. At Cotehele, all grain had to be ground at Sir Richard's mill down by the river, with the miller keeping a share of each villager's flour for the Lord of the Manor.

The fireplace in the kitchen at Cotehele is over ten feet wide and the huge oven is over seven feet across and three feet high – its dome shape is the same as those used by the Romans.

When meat was boiled it was cooked in a cauldron in a bag made from the gut of a freshly killed animal (as haggis is sold today), or in a sealed-down pottery jar. Often vegetables or puddings in other bags were cooked at the same time. At **Hampton Court Palace** in Surrey Henry VIII had a cauldron large enough to boil a whole ox.

## Good times, bad times

It is much more difficult to find out what the poor ate, as they could neither read nor write and left no accounts. Nevertheless we know that most people lived in the country, produced their own food and bartered or sold anything that was left. If the harvest was spoilt by rain they resorted to eating things like ground acorns and cats, dogs and rats for meat. When the harvest went well, their food was simple: pottage with a few vegetables and herbs, coarse bread, hard cheese, whey (which was drunk, while milk tended to be used for cheesemaking), eggs, some bacon, and occasionally a chicken, rabbit, or fish poached from the river. Nearly every cottager had a garden **(garth)** attached to his cottage, in which he grew onions, garlic, leeks, cabbage, parsnips and turnips. Beans for the pottage were probably grown on strips of land assigned to them in the common fields of the village.

# Tudor feasts

The sixteenth century was the age of exploration. Adventurers from Spain, Portugal, France, Holland and England would set off to unknown lands in their ships, returning with exciting finds, including food.

## Market gardens

Later in the century the Low Countries – now Holland and Belgium – became part of the Spanish Empire and religious quarrels broke out between the Protestant Dutch and the Catholic Spanish. Refugees from Holland fled to England, bringing with them their skills as market gardeners, and set up nurseries to grow vegetables on the outskirts of cities. In London, for instance, the Hackney turnip and the Fulham parsnip became famous.

But some people thought these root crops were unhealthy to eat because they were grown in earth. Rich people, moreover, felt that vegetables were for the poor and stuck to a diet of mainly meat, fish and sweets. Look at the Tudor feast menu on page 16, for instance. High-born Tudors, including Henry VIII himself, may have had poorly-balanced diets and suffered from diseases like scurvy because of a lack of fresh fruit and vegetables.

## Foreign origins

From the Americas came some of the most exciting new foods, like the potato, which was originally regarded as poisonous and used as a decorative flower. Only in the eighteenth century did it become an important part of the English everyday diet. Turkeys, domesticated by the American Indians from the 1520s, also made their way on to the English table.

## A grand hostess

In the 1590s Bess of Hardwick, who lived at **Hardwick Hall** in Derbyshire, was one of the richest people in England and kept a magnificent house. She had two rooms for entertaining: the larger and grander was the High Great Chamber – the most sumptuously furnished in the whole house. Bess dined in great ceremony in this room. She and her honoured guests sat on chairs, while everybody else had stools. When not in use, the silver plate was displayed on shelves with a cupboard below – this piece of furniture was called a court dresser.

By this time the wealthy no longer ate in the hall, except on very special occasions. It would continue to be used by servants but the family would take their meals in a more private room.

At Hardwick, the food would be brought in a formal procession from the kitchen through the hall (where everyone present stood up in its honour), up the two flights of the staircase and finally into the Great Chamber. The dinner was of two courses, each consisting of several different dishes all served at once. After this came an elaborate dessert course called a 'banquet'. The menu might have been something like the one on the opposite page.

HARDWICK HALL, DERBYSHIRE

# Menu

## First Course

Pottage of stewed broth
Baked pies of calves' feet
Baked spiced custard pies
Baked quince pies
Whole side of roast beef
Boiled rabbits with puddings in their bellies
Spiced salt beef
Baked cranes and bustards

## Second Course

Roast lambs
Baked venison tarts
White puddings of hog's liver
Baked sparrow and other small birds
Open tarts of damsons
Junkets
Baked rabbits with fruit
Roast pheasant, snipe and plovers

## Banqueting houses

After the guests had finished eating the first two courses, they would retire to take the last course, the banquet, either in the Long Gallery, or in one of the specially constructed banqueting houses. There were four of these at Hardwick, including one in the garden and another on the huge flat roof, from which magnificent views could be enjoyed. The banquet was a sweet course, almost a meal in itself, eaten off specially carved wooden trenchers called 'roundels' decorated with witty sayings. Delicacies included preserved fruits and flowers, fruit-flavoured stiff jellies and sugar pastes, biscuit-type confections, milk jellies, sugar-covered spices and dark gingerbread, accompanied by sweet wines and spiced hippocras.

New trade routes had increased the import of sugar into England, thus it was possible to make many more sweet foods.

# Stuart exotics

In 1672 Elizabeth, Countess of Dysart, married the Duke of Lauderdale and set about modernising her family house, **Ham House** just outside London in Surrey. The house has survived almost unchanged so here we can see an almost perfect example of how a wealthy family lived at the end of the seventeenth century.

## Imported food

Trading links established with all parts of the world gave wealthy landowners like the Lauderdales new choices in fruit and vegetables. The walled kitchen gardens and orchard at Ham were therefore laid out with new varieties of apples, pears, plums, cherries, gooseberries, raspberries and strawberries, etc.

Glasshouses were built for exotic peaches, nectarines and apricots. Orange and lemon trees introduced into England in the seventeenth century were grown in huge terracotta pots in special rooms called 'orangeries'. Melons and pineapples were raised in 'hot beds' where the earth was kept warm by pipes from a stove. A wide variety of vegetables were also grown: endive, spinach, beetroot, asparagus, artichokes, cucumber (called Cowcumber) and pumpkins. Books were published giving advice on fruit and vegetable cultivation.

## Domestic offices

The rooms for preparing food at Ham included larders for weighing, preserving and storing food, a bakehouse where bread, biscuits and pies were baked, a dairy where cream, butter and cheese were made, a still-house for making preserves, syrups and medicines, and cellars, a scullery and a kitchen. The kitchen contained some of the most up-to-date equipment including a mechanical 'spit jack', which turned the meat without the necessity of a spit boy, and a charcoal-burning 'stewing' stove for cooking light stews or sauces.

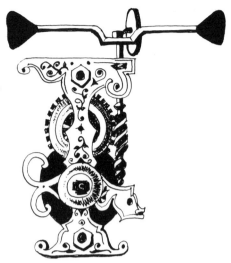

MECHANICAL SPIT JACK

Smaller quantities of food were also cooked in saucepans on a 'brigg' (a horizontal framework above the top firebars), or on a 'trivet' (an iron three-legged stand put in front of the fire on which a small saucepan could stand).

ORANGERY

## Designer dinner parties

When they were entertaining, the Lauderdales would eat in the Great Dining Room. The table was laid with a white damask cloth folded so as to leave an elaborate pattern of creases. The dishes, too, were placed on the table in a formal geometric pattern. Blocks were often put under the cloth so that dishes could be displayed in tiers. People sometimes complained that they could hardly see their neighbour across the table on festive occasions.

## A new implement

By 1670 silver forks had become a necessity in any fashionable household. The Italians had used them to eat with for many years, but Englishmen had thought them effeminate, using them only for serving food. The design of the knife changed with the introduction of the fork. As people started to use forks rather than knives to spear food, so the end of the knife became rounded.

Food was eaten off silver plates, pewter or finely painted blue-and-white pottery called Delftware. The fashionable hour for dining had moved later, to two o'clock in the afternoon. Sweet and savoury foods were still served together in the first two courses, but the last dessert course was now eaten at the dining-room table instead of withdrawing to another room. Supper, of one course, was served in the early evening at Ham and if the Lauderdales were entertaining, they might sit drinking and smoking the now fashionable tobacco, while listening to music after the meal. Before leaving, guests would be given another light meal, or at least a warming drink, such as spiced hot wine.

## Sweet tooth

Sweet puddings were now a great favourite, made easier by the invention earlier in the century of the pudding cloth which replaced pudding bags of animal gut. The cook sent up a delightful array of hot, nutritious puddings which were made with flour, eggs, butter, milk, sugar, suet, marrow, dried fruit, rice and spices.

Cakes as we know them today made their appearance at this time, with yeast so they could rise. New types of biscuit included 'jumbals' (caraway-flavoured dough moulded into rings, knots or plaits), and Shrewsbury Cakes (spiced shortcake).

Another new sweet dish was ice-cream, introduced from France and Italy in the 1650s.

## Ice houses

Ice houses were built in the grounds of great houses to preserve the ice, taken from frozen lakes and rivers during the winter. In this way it could last all through the summer months. The houses were either sunk in a pit or enclosed in earth, with hollow, straw-filled walls. Though it is of a much later date, there is a good example of an ice house at Ham.

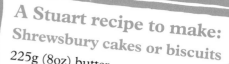

### A Stuart recipe to make:
**Shrewsbury cakes or biscuits**

225g (8oz) butter

225g (8oz) caster sugar

450g (1lb) plain flour

$\frac{1}{2}$ tsp grated nutmeg

1 tsp rosewater

1 egg

Rub the butter into the dry ingredients, then work in the egg and rosewater to form a stiff dough (add a little more water if too stiff). Roll out the dough until about $\frac{1}{2}$ cm thick, then cut out circles (about 10cms in diameter) with a pastry cutter or cup. Make a criss-cross pattern on the surface, then prick the centre of each diamond shape with a skewer. Transfer the biscuits to baking sheets and bake at gas Mark 4, 350 °F (180 °C) for 20 minutes. Remove from sheets with a spatula and cool on wire rack. This recipe makes about 8 biscuits.

ICE HOUSE
POWIS CASTLE, POWYS

**Other National Trust ice houses:**

Killerton, Devon

Attingham Park, Shropshire

Blickling Hall, Norfolk

Castle Coole, County Fermanagh

Hatchlands, Surrey

Kedleston Hall, Derbyshire

# Hot drinks

Three non-alcoholic drinks – coffee, chocolate and tea – introduced in the mid-seventeenth century were to have an important effect on English life. The first coffee house was opened in Oxford in 1650, followed soon after by several in London. They became popular meeting places, where men could discuss everything from business and politics to the latest scandal. The coffee beans were ground in a pestle and mortar: coffee grinders did not arrive in England until the end of the century.

People also drank coffee and chocolate at home, served in either coffee or chocolate pots. Chocolate was only for the rich and fashionable, priced expensively at 10 to 15 shillings per pound. It was sold in hunks, to be grated and melted in hot water. Chocolate pots usually had a small hole in the lid through which to insert a special instrument called a 'moliquet', for stirring any lumps. Chocolate and coffee were drunk without milk or sugar.

Tea was imported from China and first sold in coffee houses. Like coffee and chocolate, it was very expensive and enjoyed by rich ladies who took it in the afternoon, between lunch and dinner. The first teapots were made of silver, as only the rich could afford to drink tea, and specially made small silver teaspoons were needed to stir the tiny teacups. Teacups first came to this country as ballast on ships importing tea from the East – that is to fill up space and balance the cargo! They had no handles because that was the Chinese style. (Teacups with a single handle were made in Europe from the early 1700s). This cheap Eastern porcelain became extremely popular and it was not long before the traditional Chinese designs were the height of fashion in Britain. Small amounts of sweet food were served as an accompaniment, beginning the idea of 'afternoon tea'. The East India Company increased trade between Britain and the East, bringing more tea from China to the six-monthly auction sales in London. By 1750 it had become the most popular drink of all classes, and china tea-sets with traditional Chinese designs became highly fashionable.

# Eighteenth-century revolutions

During the eighteenth century, dramatic changes took place in the way Britain farmed and produced food. The agricultural enclosures of land meant that poor people could no longer grow their crops on the old strip system, nor graze their animals on 'common' land. They were forced instead to move to towns to find work, causing the urban population to grow very fast.

Previously towns had been small enough for their population to live off the land in the neighbouring countryside, with food brought in daily to busy markets. The rapid growth of towns now made this difficult: fish was often rotten and unfit to eat. People complained that vegetables from market gardens around London tasted unpleasant because of the smoke from coal fires. Meat and poultry were not so badly affected because animals were walked to market along 'drove' roads and slaughtered when they reached town.

Dairy products, too, were often unfresh in towns. Many small urban dairies kept their cows in dark, overcrowded, filthy conditions, while milkmaids carrying open pails sold their produce from door to door. Small boys frequently threw things into the pails for a joke.

In the country, in the dairies of manor houses and farms like **Townend** in Cumbria, much more attention was paid to cleanliness, in order to prevent the cream, butter and cheese from 'going off'.

TOWNEND, CUMBRIA

# A rural household

In 1748 Benjamin Browne was head of the household at Townend. Here life was less grand and formal than in the large country houses. Everyone – family, servants and farmhands – sat together at the long oak table in the kitchen to eat their meals.

Mrs Browne would have had one or two maids, but she would also have contributed her share of the household work. Rising early, she might have started by helping in the dairy to make butter or cheese. The majority of utensils at this period – butter prints, cheese moulds, bowls, buckets, skeels (short-handled ladles) – were carved from sycamore wood which had a clean, white appearance and did not warp or crack. Cheese-making was a long and difficult process requiring skill and patience. Butter-making was a quicker process, but the churning to turn cream into butter was hard work. The churn used by Mrs Browne was the plunger type, which had been in use for hundreds of years. When the butter was ready, it would often be stamped with an image, such as swans, thistles, fruit or flowers.

## Kitchen equipment

Technological discoveries in the eighteenth century made it possible to produce a better quality and wider choice of kitchen equipment. In many households like Townend the job of the unfortunate spit boy, or dog, was replaced by a clockwork jack which mechanically turned the spit evenly and slowly. Trivets, iron brackets on which to rest saucepans, were attached to the side of the fire basket and could be swung out over it when needed.

Baking was another task Mrs Browne would have supervised with her maids. In the north of England, oatmeal was used far more in baking than wheat. This, of course, affected the type of things made, such as thin oatcakes, cooked on a griddle over a peat fire. At Townend, built into the wall beside the fireplace is a carved oak cupboard for storing bread and oatcakes. Above the fireplace in the kitchen rises the meat loft. Here the hams, bacon and sausages hung to be slowly smoked.

Food at Townend would have been fairly simple, but of good quality: breakfast of oatcakes, butter, cold meat and cheese, with ale or tea to drink. (Tea was no longer prohibitively expensive.) A normal dinner might be boiled beef with cabbage, a pigeon pie, rice pudding and gooseberry pie.

## Ovens and water heaters

Huge kitchen fires were gradually enclosed and made smaller. At first the oven was made of iron rather than brick, with a grate underneath, called the 'perpetual oven'. Later, the oven and main fire were combined, with a water boiler and tap added to the opposite side from the oven, so that for the first time hot water was on tap. By the end of the century, the fire was also covered over and the first patent for a 'closed range' was taken out in 1802.

## A country house

A house that shows how the wealthy lived in the eighteenth century is **Kedleston Hall** in Derbyshire. The kitchen, like the rest of the house, was designed down to the smallest detail by the great classical architect, Robert Adam, so that grand visitors could look down from the gallery. Rows of ordered pots and pans give some idea of the labour that went into cooking elaborate meals for Lord Scarsdale, owner of Kedleston, and his family. Meat was still roasted in front of the fire on a huge mechanical spit, but smaller joints could be cooked in the 'Dutch oven', a rounded, open-fronted metal box, highly polished inside to reflect the heat from the fire. A bottle-jack, on which meat was hung, was mounted inside, and there was a door in the back for basting.

The dining-room at Kedleston is a fine example of up-to-date ideas on dining held by eighteenth-century men of taste. Robert Adam ensured that the paintings and decoration of the room referred in some way to food and drink. The figures on the fireplace are Ceres and Bacchus, Roman gods of harvest and wine, while the panels on the wall represent the four seasons. At the end of the dining-room is a semi-circular domed alcove designed to hold Lord Scarsdale's collection of plate, silver wine fountains, canteens (boxes for precious silver knives), a candelabra-like object for burning perfume, and a plate warmer disguised as a piece of sculpture.

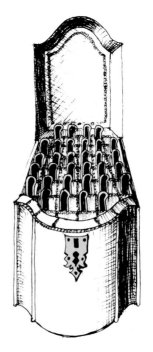

## Seating plans

Normally the chairs were placed round the walls, to be brought forward and tables carried in only at meal times. Guests entered in strict order of rank, ladies first. Ladies and gentlemen were beginning to sit alternately, instead of all the ladies at one end of the table and all the men at the other. Some men complained about this, fearing women would make meals more sensible and less boisterous.

# Formal dinner

It was still the custom to serve two courses with several dishes in each course. The first usually consisted of soup, followed by a fish dish, and then meats, roasted, boiled, stewed and fried, some with sauces. Little dishes of biscuits and pickles were put on the table and bread was handed round. The second course was made up of lighter dishes of meat and fish, plus several sweet pies, puddings and tarts.

Dessert followed the second course, with jellies, sweetmeats, fruit, nuts and cheese. After this had been removed the ladies withdrew into another room, while the men remained drinking port, madeira and brandy. These meals were so substantial that breakfast, taken between 10 and 11am, became a smaller meal with fine white bread or toast taken with tea, coffee or chocolate.

## A rich pudding to make:
### Syllabub

This pudding recipe dates from the seventeenth century, taking its name from the part of France where the wine called 'sill' came from, and the Elizabethan slang word 'bub' – a bubbling drink. The wine used to be added to frothing cream, but a simpler version can be made with lemon juice.

200g (7oz) caster sugar

2 tablespoons chopped almonds

finely grated peel of 2 lemons

600ml (1 pint) double cream

Grate the lemon rind with as little of the white as possible. Mix together with juice and leave for about an hour. Pour in the cream and whisk until it just stays solid when piled up. Spoon into tall glasses or small glass dishes and scatter nuts on the top. Chill and serve several hours later.

This recipe makes 4 helpings.

# Victorian formality

The nineteenth century saw great improvements in transport, with the advent of the railways and network of canals. Food could be transported more quickly and therefore freshly into the fast-developing towns, improving the diet of the better off and, to a certain extent, of the poor. Adulteration – falsifying food by adding inferior ingredients – decreased, though people continued to add water to milk, floor sweepings or sand to tea, and chalk and plaster to flour.

## Mass-produced food

Increasingly food was being processed and packaged in new 'manufactories'. In 1847 the first large meat-canning factory was set up in Australia, (but they didn't export much of their produce until about 1866 when the price of fresh meat had risen in Britain because of cattle disease); and in 1861 the first cheese factory opened in Derbyshire. Liquid yeast, slow and messy to use, was replaced by quick-acting compressed yeast, which, together with self-raising flour and baking powder, revolutionised the time taken to bake. Custard made from fresh eggs and cream was superseded by powder produced by Bird's.

## At your service

At a great nineteenth-century country houses like **Penrhyn Castle** in North Wales, most of the food cooked for the Pennant family and their servants continued to be brought in on a daily basis. For the times, the household was moderate in size: in 1883 twenty-three women servants and eighteen men. Unlike the medieval household, where the majority of servants were men, by Victorian times, most of the inside servants were women.

Another medieval characteristic, master and servant spending a large part of their lives together, had also long gone. There was a strict hierarchy amongst the servants. The housekeeper and the butler were the most senior, followed by the first lady's maid and first footman, down to the youngest scullery maid and the 'odd man', who did all the odd jobs.

## Below stairs

Despite the moderate size of the household staff, the rooms where food was produced at Penrhyn are complex. In the pastry room the table tops are made of Welsh slate to keep the pastry cool while being worked. The kitchen too uses local slate as a hygienic surround for the huge range (the Pennant family owned the mines). All the dirty jobs were undertaken in the scullery next door: washing and peeling vegetables and cleaning fish and game. Dirty dishes were washed with piped water in the big wooden sinks.

Beyond the courtyard stands the bakehouse for bread-making, and the brewhouse for beer and ale. In the same courtyard is the ice tower, where ice was brought up each winter from the River Ogwen and shovelled into the twenty-three-foot deep pit which was lined with brick and straw to maintain the low temperature. Ice was cut into blocks and taken inside, to be packed into zinc- or tin-lined boxes. Food was then put on top and sealed in. This ice tower made possible the manufacture of iced puddings, ice creams and sorbets – very fashionable in Victorian times. They were usually made in elaborate moulds, then decorated with fresh fruit and biscuits.

### A Victorian pudding to make:
#### Hedgehog

This was a very popular and traditional sweet dish for the well-off in Victorian times. More complicated versions of the recipe were made using sponge cake and rum or sherry.

450g (1lb) prunes in syrup

225g (8oz) blanched almonds

1 lemon jelly

1 lime jelly

an oval jelly mould

Pour the prunes and the syrup into a saucepan, add sugar and stew over a gentle heat for about 10 minutes. When they have cooled, cut into quarters taking out the stones; keep the juice in the pan. Make the lemon jelly, following the instructions on the packet but using the prune juice made up with water to 400ml (3/4 pint) – pour into an oval mould. Stir in the prunes and leave to set. When nearly set make up the green jelly and keep in the pan. When the lemon jelly has set turn it out on a flat dish and stick almonds all over to make the hedgehog's spikes (leave one end uncovered for the head). Now pour the half-set green jelly all round the edge to look like grass and put the dish in the refrigerator. Just before serving sprinkle sugar on the green grass to look like snow.

## Continental flavour

Penrhyn followed the style of most great houses of the time where the food was made to French recipes. Menu cards set out on the tables were written in French, even if the dish was English. This tradition continues in many English restaurants today.

Why not make your own menu card for a special meal at home.

## Breakfast

By 1850 breakfast at a grand house like Penrhyn would generally be a fairly informal meal, taken between 9 and 11am. Hot dishes, such as eggs, sausages, fish, bacon and sometimes even game birds would be put into silver 'chafing' dishes with lids to keep them warm. The sideboard would also be set out with cold ham, potted meats and perhaps a cold meat pie. Hot bread rolls and scones fresh from the bakehouse were laid out with home-made jams and marmalades. Lastly there might be some stewed fruit with cream. Tea and coffee were offered to drink.

## Making an entrance

Evening dinner was held at 7 or 7.30 pm. Guests were expected to dress formally, men in black tail coats, ladies in elaborate gowns. Pre-dinner drinks – aperitifs – were quaffed in one room and then each lady was taken down to the dining-room by a gentleman, who then sat beside them. The tables were splendidly decorated by fruit and flowers brought in daily by the head gardener and displayed on epergnes, magnificent centrepieces.

## The order changeth

One of the most important changes in nineteenth-century dining customs was the service of the food. Meals had always been served with all the different dishes together, but by 1850 the English were following the French and serving dishes in order with every dish divided up and a helping served to each guest. The meal was thus made of many smaller courses, known as 'Russian service'.

## A Victorian bishop's mitre napkin design

1. Lay napkin out in front of you.

2. Fold in half, straight side to straight side.

3. Take top right corner and fold down to centre of base fold.

4. Take bottom left corner and bring up to meet at the top.

5. Turn napkin over so folds are now face down.

6. Take top edge and fold down to meet bottom edge, leaving flaps loose.

7. Take bottom right corner and fold in under the flap on the left side, making sure that it fits right into the edge for a snug fit.

8. Turn over. Again take bottom right hand corner and fold in under the flap on the left side.

9. Now stand napkin up and gently shape into a round as below.

## Last but not least

Another innovation was the introduction of the savoury. This was a small, strong-tasting dish, such as anchovies or mushrooms on toast, eaten after the dessert. Savouries were regarded as manly, and so were not usually eaten by the ladies, who left after the coffee was served, so that the gentlemen could drink their port.

# Edwardian elegance

astle Drogo in Devon was built from 1910 for Julius Drewe by the distinguished architect Edwin Lutyens. Drewe was one of the businessmen responsible for some of the great changes in food retailing that took place in the late nineteenth century.

CASTLE DROGO
DEVON

## Enough for everyone

Between 1851 and 1911 the population of Britain had doubled to thirty-six million. A large number of people had moved from the country into the towns, greatly increasing the demand for food. Even though the number of shops also increased, they could not cope with the amount of cheap imported foods flooding into the country. A completely new form of distribution made its appearance: 'multiple shop retailing' – the origin of our modern supermarkets. By buying imported foods cheaply in bulk and selling them through a network of shops (like Sainsburys or Tesco today) these companies were able to keep prices low. Clever advertising was used for the first time to help to sell food. The results were so successful that these new retailers became very rich. Julius Drewe, who founded the Home & Colonial Stores, became so prosperous that he retired aged thirty-three and searched for an appropriate country house. This was to be Castle Drogo.

# Electric power

Although a little more modest in size, life in this house was not so different from Penrhyn Castle. There were plenty of servants, a fine kitchen garden brought in fresh fruit and vegetables daily, and food was luxurious and plentiful. Certain major changes made life easier for the servants. Castle Drogo was one of the 2% of houses in 1910 to have electricity. It may have had an electric kettle (first made in England in 1902), an electric refrigerator (available since 1907). Luxury packaged foods were also available, such as tinned oysters, tongue (a great favourite) foreign fruits, bottled sauces and chutneys, Bovril, Cadbury's cocoa and some cereals such as cornflakes.

The kitchen and other domestic rooms at Castle Drogo were beautifully laid out by Lutyens. He even designed the huge plate racks, draining board and a giant pestle and mortar.

CASTLE DROGO, DEVON

## Gadgets

The array of kitchen utensils changed in the 1880s when tin-plated mechanical labour-saving devices were introduced. These included graters, potato peelers, mincers, apple corers, slicers and cake tins.

MINCER

APPLE CORER

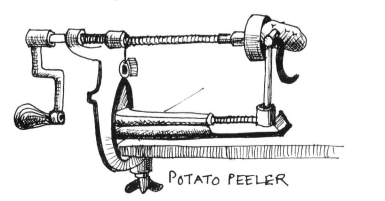

POTATO PEELER

## Saving time

The new electric and gas cookers, refrigerators and other kitchen appliances of the early twentieth century made cooking and preparing food less time consuming. As more time-saving devices were invented – such as electric food processors – so meal times became more flexible. Today we can buy instant meals which are ready in minutes in a microwave oven.

**31**

# Other National Trust kitchens to visit

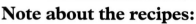

### Buckland Abbey,
#### Yelverton, Devon

Kitchen contains open hearths and a bread oven dating back to Elizabethan times, plus charcoal ovens and utensils from the eighteenth century.

### Charlecote Park,
#### Wellesbourne, Warwickshire

Mid-nineteenth-century kitchens, plus a bakehouse and brewhouse.

### Dunham Massey,
#### Altrincham, Cheshire

Kitchens with several kinds of ovens and mainly nineteenth-century furniture, plus a servery, butler's pantry, larders and sculleries.

### East Riddlesden Hall,
#### Keighley, Yorkshire

Seventeenth-century kitchen with unusual gadgets like the oatcake roller and sugar nippers.

### Florence Court,
#### Enniskillen, Co. Fermanagh

Kitchens and many other rooms for preparing food, including a jam house, a china store, and a potato house.

### Saltram,
#### Plympton, Devon

The Great Kitchen, separate from the main house, contains many eighteenth-century gadgets and utensils, including copper pans and turning spits.

### Shugborough,
#### Milford, Staffordshire

Nineteenth-century kitchens and brewhouse restored to working order; demonstrations are given to show how servants worked here. You can also watch bread being baked in the flour mill and traditional cheese – and butter-making in the dairy on the home farm.

### Speke Hall,
#### Liverpool, Merseyside

Fully-equipped Victorian kitchen plus a servants' hall dating back to the sixteenth century.

### Tatton Park,
#### Knutsford, Cheshire

Nineteenth-century kitchens, larders, still-rooms, plus a housekeeper's room and a range of cellars.

## Note about the recipes:

There are two kinds of recipe in this book. One type shows you what kind of food was eaten at different periods in history – these are NOT to be tried at home; the others are practical recipes that you can make, by following the cooking instructions.

First published in 1992 by National Trust Enterprises, 36 Queen Anne's Gate, London SW1H 9AS

Registered Charity No. 205846

ISBN 0 7078 0149 4

Designed by Blade Communications, Leamington Spa

Printed in Hong Kong by Wing King Tong